ABOUT THE ANTHOLOGY

Setting out to create this anthology we knew it would be near enough impossible to capture the magic, spirit and energy of Poetry Jam. But we wanted to try.

Poetry Jam was established to create inclusive spaces where people could explore their ideas, philosophies and their relationships to others as well as the city.

We see this anthology as an extension of those principles creating a tangible permanent space to mark the incredible talent we have in this city we call home.

Poetry Jam has evolved in the past five years, since opening its doors to 40 people at Urban Coffee Company in 2013, and has surpassed our expectations in terms of its importance, relevance and resonance with young people and the wider community alike.

We are honoured to be able to celebrate this milestone with all of you; the poets, the audience, the writers, the baristas, the people of Birmingham.

This one's for you.

Wild Dreams
And Louder Voices
The Poetry Jam Anthology

VERVE
POETRY PRESS
BIRMINGHAM

PUBLISHED BY VERVE POETRY PRESS
C/O 40, St Nicholas Avenue, Kenilworth, Warks.
www.vervepoetrypress.com

All rights reserved
© 2018 all individual authors

The right of all individuals to be identified as author if this work has been asserted in accordance with section 77 of the Copyright, Designs and Patents Act 1988.

No part of this work may be reproduced, stored or transmitted in any form or by any means, graphic, electronic, recorded or mechanical, without the prior written permission of the publisher.

FIRST PUBLISHED FEB 2018

Printed in the UK by TJ International

ISBN: 978-1-912565-00-9

*Poetry Jam belongs to you,
to me, to us
and to everyone who hasn't
found their way here yet.*

CONTENTS

Foreword by Polarbear

Introduction by Anisa Haghdadi

Be Beautiful - Amerah Saleh	15
Brown Girl - Nadia Ghazan	18
The Honour Of Animals - Polarbear	19
A Job's Not Who You Are – Spoz Poet	21
Birthday Cake - Kavita Kler	22
Read My Lips - Deanna Rodger	23
Mourning - Nyanda Foday	25
Jour Après Jour - Lexia Tomlinson	26
Black British Girl - Saidatu Odutayo	27
My Body Is My Home - Dawn Grant	30
Skater Girl - Casey Bailey	31
Spare Change - Leon Priestnall	32
Ten (X) - Scarlett Ward	33
Leaving The Nest - Ariya Larker	35
The In-Between Date - Nafeesa Hamid	37
Liberation - Yasmina Silva	38

Reunion - Leah Atherton	39
Future Clothes - Livi Pilkington	41
Maleena - Ahsen Sayeed	43
Dis Black Womanhood - Amara Ranger	47
Noise - Dennis Muhirwa Nkurunziza	48
Brown Voices Amongst White Noises - Aliyah Begum	51
Number 6 - Kamil Mahmood	52
Hobbies Include: - Hannah Swings	53
Withering - Adjei Dsane	54
My Friend's Grandmother Is A Socialist - Ahlaam Moledina	55
Monday The 11th of December 2017. 21:05 - Ciona Nankervis	56
Extinct - Jasmine Gardosi	57
Gentrification Poem - Joe Cook	59
Her (v2) - Seunfunmi E. Tinubu	61
Theatre Is Not For Us - Jacob Crutchley & Zeddie	63
The Jam - Sipho Eric Dube	70

Notes & Acknowledgements

FOREWORD

I am from Birmingham.

Wherever I go in the world, that fact makes me feel strong.

I have been lucky enough to find a voice in my work, and to know how empowering that feels.

Through writing, sharing, listening and collaborating, I feel like my creative pursuits allow me to figure out my ongoing journey through this crazy gameshow we call existence.

Anyone who has ever created something and shared it with an audience, or been part of an audience where something spoke to them, knows how powerful that can be. It is the crackling risk of sharing part of yourself and the solid sense of genuine connection that can follow.

It is not a complicated thing, but there are not always enough spaces or opportunities for it to occur.

Birmingham is a funny place.

Birmingham is that person you know who is amazing at that thing, who you know dreams of sharing it with the world, but doesn't, for fear of embarrassment or ridicule, or of basically being told it's not good enough. The joke of it is, just like that person, underneath that fear, Birmingham knows it's incredible. Birmingham just needs a little push, at the right moment, to open a door, take a risk, or simply be given a safe space to share. Set up a night where people can.

And look what happens.

When Anisa set up Poetry Jam, it was because she wanted to create a space for that connection. A connection she had felt and wanted more of, for herself and for others. She took a risk in hoping that other people felt the same.

And man, didn't they just?

What Poetry Jam and Beatfreeks Collective do makes me happy. What they are doing, have done and will do even more,

is represent Birmingham's brilliance.
And I love Birmingham.
I love it in the same way that you love a big sister. That way where you have your own in jokes. That way where just a look is enough to communicate everything. That way where you don't always get along. Can push each others buttons. That way where once in a while you out and out fight and don't see each other for a bit. But that way in which, underneath everything that happens, you trust your love enough, beyond anything, to feel a strength from it deep in your gut that encourages connection and propels you to be who you are.
And what's more important than that?

Nothing.
Nothing is.

Nice one

Steven (Polarbear). 2018

INTRODUCTION

I remember falling in love with spoken word.

Cassie and Kesha performed a couple of pieces at a show I was putting on at the library theatre as a teenager and a fire started in my belly. I was left moved, inspired, angry and nourished all in one and I felt like my soul had been given a hug. I was sold. I started creating more spaces to platform more young poets like Cassie and Kesha and even began 'bedroom writing'. At the same time, I was playing with a new idea; a social enterprise that could cradle young people's stories, empower communities and make an impact on the city I'd chosen to commit to. Birmingham. But I never imagined what came next.

Fast forward to February 2013 and I'm nervously heading into Urban Coffee Company on Church Street not knowing if anyone will come to the first Poetry Jam which I had only promoted a couple of weeks before. People were already there. People wanting to perform and those wanting to listen. The movement was in motion. The people I met, the poetry I witnessed, changed the course of my life. It created the space for a new community to form. Without Poetry Jam I wouldn't have met some of my team, and some of my closest friends; people who believed in the vision and supported me to realise it. This is dedicated to them.

This anthology represents more than poetry in the city, it's about young voices, old and new being in a space that they feel valued, encouraged and listened to. It wasn't designed to reach it's 5th birthday or to publish poets. It's wasn't designed to grow at all! It was designed on extremely simple but powerful principles; ones that have guided us til today.

Poetry Jam is a space for people, especially young people, to take ownership of their space, their ideas, their experiences and their city. It's us reclaiming our stories, healing, deconstructing and renewing. It's philosophy, rebellion and relief when we need it most.

To the Poetry Jam community; this is dedicated to you. Thank you for making the night yours.

x

Anisa Haghdadi
Founder & CEO
The Beatfreeks Collective

Wild Dreams
And Louder Voices

Be Beautiful
Amerah Saleh

What you define as beautiful is only your perception.
Maybe you've been blinded to what beauty really means.
I need you to close your eyes.
I don't need you to define it to me,
but look in the mirror.
And through the dirty broken bits realise your heart is
imprinted in their edges.
And they fit,
so perfectly.

Let your weary heart tell people it has got space for them.
It doesn't need to speak,
Let them feel it.
Understand your soul.
Your posture tells the world you're a soldier fighting a war you
don't even know you're going into.
And that makes you double the soldier they assume you to be.

Stand.
Stand like bullets go straight through you.
Stand like you're defending a lover, a brother, a sister or a
mother.
Stand like you're defending yourself because you care.
And that's okay.

Let your soul linger in places like the good food you smell and
know what it is straight away.
Let them say your name when you're not there.

Your attire
is as casual,
formal

or scruffy as you allow it to be.
If your intentions are ugly
no amount of makeup can hide it.
It'll seep through your skin that you bleed out of and appear as a red flash.
And in the spark that's meant to be there
it'll be clear.

Your eyes
Your eyes can hide the world's problems
But your eyes can't hide your love, passion, your humility or the compassion in you
It'll glow.
Be that in the dark or in the light
It'll shine bright.
Brighter.

Your feet surrender the pushing you mentally give yourself.
Be better.
Be helpful
Be cool
Be nice
Be thoughtful
Be thought provoking
Be there
Everywhere at once
But when your feet stop and the seconds on the clocks keep ticking
It's time..
You need a break.
Rest your feet and watch the magic you helped create.
You don't have to be there to know that your presence is.

Your arms are out of reach for you to hold.
So hold onto someone else's.
Don't let pride hide you away from arms that are trying to calm your soul.

Hug tight.
Tighter.
Hug like it's your last because it could be.
Someone hug me so tight it'll break every single one of my ribs, clench my stomach in.
BREAK ME WITH A HUG.

Follow your dreams.
Stop sleeping in until late afternoon trying to chase them whilst your eyes are closed.
There are people hungry for the same thing and if you're unable to see it
they'll go for it
just like that.
Run, chase, run so fast there's no more oxygen around to keep you running.

STOP.
Stop tiring yourself out with questions of why you're doing what you're doing.
Write me your story,
Sing me the melody of your unbalance.
Dance me a choreographed piece of your future.
Film me your family.
Take a picture of your tragedy.
Draw me your strengths and weaknesses.
Paint me your doubts and sorrows.
Then place them on your wall.
Cross off one each day.
Sit in your space.
Spend time with family, friends, strangers, homeless men.
Explore their stories.
Be compassionate.
Open your eyes.
Be beautiful:
Because as cliché as it sounds you are the only person in this world that can be your kind of beautiful.

Brown Girl
Nadia Ghazan

Brown girl is the richness of her Mother's cooking;
She burns like chilli and she is as unexpected as the
Flavour of cardamom
She has no precise measurable recipe and she is,
Most definitely, too much for a simple palate.

Brown girl is soft decorated hands the colour
Of the wheat grown in her Mother's village-
Hands so soft, kissed, by her foremothers;
Women who crafted homes amongst mountains-
Raised children amongst war.

Brown girl is the woven carpets of her homeland;
Walk over her in haste and you will skip over
The tales intricately stitched between her lines but look
Closely and you'll hear the whispers of lands inaccessible to
those
Who do not know their winding mountain paths
Like their own Mother's name.

Brown girl is a river of flowing hair so thick that
It will break free of hair bands just as she breaks
Free of your stereotypes - brown girl is brown arms
Kissed with black hair and strong enough to carry well water
For miles - Brown girl's hips; difficult to squeeze into jeans
Wide enough to birth eight children and carry her grandchild.

Brown girl was the music of your homeland and,
Whilst you may have forgotten her words,
Her melody will stick to you like
The smell of garlands tied around your neck.

The Honour Of Animals
Polarbear

Kneeling on the balding bedroom carpet
in my school shirt and trousers
and an old black tie
nose pressed against the glass watching
uncle Joe and another man take turns
to fully punch each other in the face.
I'm 10. It's my first proper funeral.
It's almost like they're dancing.
Both of them stood, in their cheap suits
on the patchy back lawn, crunching their fists
into each other's faces.
One punch at a time.
Neither of them going down.
Nan and mom and a bunch of cousins I've never met before
are all down stairs, crammed into the living room
around a dead body.
I can hear Louis Armstrong's 'We have all the time in the
World'.
Each one punches, then waits and takes one
like a conversation.

Less than an hour later I'm sitting
in the kitchen watching them two,
sat in the corner, laughing.
Turns out they're brothers.
Two brothers sat laughing and swigging cans
through split lips on purple mouths,
spitting out stories of schoolboy beatings,
their eyes swollen shut,
hands like bags of broken stone.

The honour of animals.
The spark in my gut.
I can't help it.
It's genes. I'm predisposed.
Predisposed to the romance of a broken nose.

A Job's Not Who You Are
Spoz Poet

For twenty five years I was that man.
That man who'd get up some time after six
And take his biggest risk - cornflakes or wheetabix?
That man who fell out of bed and fell into work,
Fell for the Rover, over the Merc and the Beamer
Cause they were for dreamers.
That man who'd got the beautiful house,
The beautiful wife, the beautiful kids,
I was a genius - yeah you should have seen us.
Happy with my lot and everything I'd got,
That I'd worked for with my job, called a career,
The something that was getting me there from here.

But I never got there.
Me and five thousand ex-Rover colleagues never got there,
Where ever there was,
We know it isn't fair, Spoz,
Our hands are tied, the management lied,
Now don't scream and shout,
But the light at the end of the tunnel's gone out.

Understatement - I was dazed
Understatement - I was confused
Understatement - I was in shock
But I was no stick of rock.
Cut me in half and it didn't say Rover it was over.
Yes, I was punch drunk, yes, I was floored,
But it was time to sever that umbilical cord.
Find a new identity - the one I knew I was meant to be.

Because a job isn't who you are - it's what you do,
There are bigger things in life that define the likes of me and you,

Like that little fishy from your dad,
The tiny egg from your mom,
A sprinkle from a miracle and the two become one,
You or me - see?
But that's just biology, it happens every day,
Because your God and my God kind of made it that way.
It's the trail you tread, not as a job but a vocation,
From every nation and global location,
That when mixed with your genes, no I.D. card can describe,
The different identities from one common tribe.

Birthday Cake
Kavita Kler

I have lived more years than
those which are signified,
by wisps of smoke
ascending over
clouds of
cream.

Read My Lips
Deanna Rodger
(Originally commissioned by Christian McLaughlin for 'Read My Lips')

CAN YOU HEAR ME?
Or am I speaking to myself
placed high on the shelf
in an invisible box as sound proof as death
mouth committed theft
stole sound so now I
sit in a world where words mean nothing so nothing is said instead
thoughts sugar coffee black space
restless as they refuse to cease pace
cos she, he and her felt like I deserved no voice
cos I made the choice to speak up once birthday luck had run out
hence why a statement morphed into a shout
which then transcribed to "get the fuck out"
So I left
and its for the best
cos when I speak I rush in and don't think
push fam to the end and mum to the brink of despair, I appear
not to care about how they feel or what they see in me
though I fear lights filtered through negativity because in minds eye
I'm the black sheep
the one that stands alone
isolated and transported to my own unique zone of imagination
a creation of mine and I don't mind
cos see its better this way
I can talk to paper and write my say
allow those hard of hearing to read and relate
it's fate, this gift of writing
cease teeth from constantly biting slug which leaves a trail

of pure slime I now lay prints of a biro'd line so eyes can trace
my rhythmical rhyme
some would call it compliance because I vent in silence try to
turn back on violence, I desire peace
though I resent the police, they do what they please
suck prime dick on knees swallow keys of equality
I don't believe they care much for micro society
merely sound absorbers
disguise lies in orders
mute two million protests to prevent governmental contest,
and as,
soundless feet
march to a beat
refused to take seat
rather stand to replace those victims of a bomb burnt land, I
realised
that advice I never listened to
was that I should always listen
unplug ears from plasticine
de-mould self from day dream
draw in breath and colour out scream
beat drum with a sound stick beamed straight to mind find key
to box unlock zips and scream the words
READ. MY. LIPS.

Mourning
Nyanda Foday

I am good at mourning.
Things I never lost,
Things I never had.
There is a sweet undernote to the bitterness of missing the person sitting next to you
The way it feels when your gut twists with the guilt.
I cry through the smiles,
Saying goodbye to ideas and ideals
And in my room I curl in on myself,
Contort my body into apologies
As I think all the things I'll never say
As if they are dead.
Sometimes my mouth is like a tombstone
And I am forced to wonder which one of us it reads for.
Perhaps I do not mourn like you are dead.
Perhaps this is how the dead mourns
For the living,
For everything still present.
Perhaps I can't reach across because I am already six feet under, or ash,
And perhaps I'm not mourning your death, but rather my lack of life,
As I am held fixed and everyone continues around me, unapologetically.
And while you speak, and laugh, and breathe,
My corpse lungs constrict around my heart
Decay claws at my throat
And I give rigor mortis smiles.
Perhaps I am not good at mourning.
Perhaps I'm just good at dying.

Jour Après Jour
Lexia Tomlinson

You're a graveyard for O-mouth-moths
So stiff-limbed you look embalmed by the light,
Parallel lines in vacuum,
So bright, so blinding.

Your parent's marriage is a dead duck floating on the bathwater of your youth. You stare at your prune wrinkled hands daily, nightly, hourly, knowing any second you could pull the plug.

But you don't and you won't.
So you inflate yourself with purpose and negative ideas about love.

If a tree falls and nobody is there to see it (you know the rest).
If a boy falls face forward into a grave of his own making will there be a woman strong enough to dig him out?

Night bleeds into day, and day back into night.
Jour après jour.
Night bleeds into day, and day back into night.
Jour après jour.
Night bleeds into day, and day back into night.
Jour après jour.

I hope you find love
      In spaces you never thought to search,
            But dug deep,
                By wreck-less-will.

And this time, hopefully, the mountain will make a meal of the sea.

Black British Girl
Saidatu Odutayo

From the age of 11, I remember having to mature so quickly. Understanding that the world around me was no playground, because people were being shot down.

Black girls had the option of being a teenage mother, set up chick, black bitch for a drug lord, a jezebel, maid, slave, or a hoe with daddy issues, having sex with any man that showed the slightest bit of attention, so that they felt love from a man.

I remember seeing girls get pregnant so young, forced to drop out of school and seeing guys walk away freely, leaving girls that looked just like me to be single mothers.

I remember quickly developing an understanding that being a black British girl came with a number of stereotypes, because as soon as people saw me they were quick to judge me for the colour of my skin. Quick to think that like those before me I may just sink.

I remember being told by teachers when I was 12 that I was an intimidating character, that when I smiled I made them feel uneasy, and when I weren't smiling I seemed angry. So, I remember avoiding eye contact with people because clearly there must have been something wrong with my ability to communicate my feelings, as each expression gave off the wrong meaning.

What I did was grow thick skin, to ensure that I was more, I gave more, said more and became more.

I'm more than the stereotype that labels me a teenage mother, a child with daddy issues, a whore, a sket, a set up chick, a gang member.

I'm more than the child of a slave, a single mother, a what-less father, a savage.

I'm MORE, because my mother taught me that I could be anything, granted I put my mind to it, and I've grown up believing one thing, 'courage is an inner resolutions to move forward despite all obstacles.'

So I may have seen my first lifeless body at the age of 11, and I may have witnessed many more drop after that, but my mind grew fat with resilience, the ability to bounce back from anything and I've done just that.

I celebrate the fact that I grew up around South-East London, where many fell into the trap of living by the sword and dying by just that, but I made it out, a Southwark youth councillor, student ambassador, a poet and now a graduate.

I plan to further celebrate by giving back to my community, allowing those younger than me to see that their so much more that they can be, more to life than what they may have seen.

I'm a strong believer that we need to celebrate the achievements of our Black British girls, who from young have been brainwashed to believe that they must sell themselves short, wear tight clothes to gain attention from men, where make up to be beautiful, told that they contour there face and wear weave to look like white girls, put down for being a light skinned black girl or a dark skinned black girl, like the shade of their skin changes the fact that they are simply beautiful girls.

So I congratulate the black girl who is a single mum, for she struggles to provide for her child.

I congratulate the black girl who overcame her daddy issues and learnt that she is worth more.

I congratulate the black girl who likes getting her weave laid and knows that even without it, in her natural glory she is beautiful.

I congratulate the black girl who found love in art, poetry, music and dance despite being told through stereotypes that she should be a doctor or lawyer.

I congratulate the black girl who broke free from the shackles of a drug lord, or the black girls still trying to break free so she can dance, I just want to praise you.

I congratulate the black women and her children who despite facing domestic violence learnt that she can fight back.

I just congratulate my black girls because additive approach put forward by Yuval Davis, holds that black women suffer 3 types of oppression, in being black, a women and a working class, but being black and a women doesn't render us working class.

So I congratulate my black girls because you are more, give more, feel more and can always be more.

I toast to my black British girls.

My Body Is My Home
Dawn Grant

This is my body,
It's my home.
The earthly abode of my ethereal soul.
I am a sacred space, to be honoured, no less,
And I deserve respect and such sweet gentleness,
As if I were the purest, most precious crystal egg,
Sparkling with sapphire and rooted in a rose of rich ruby red.

My soft innocent curves, delicately crafted in the hands of divinity,
A miracle of creation, worthy to be cradled with love and humility.
The shell that protects my nude, raw, open-hearted vulnerability,
To be cracked open and peeled with fiercely devoted sensitivity.

My inner sanctuary to be entered in peace.
So through this union with my beloved, all my fears I may release
As I surrender to the glorious power of love
As it transcends and heals through my lover's sacred touch.

Skater Girl
Casey Bailey

I know a girl who skates.
She rollerblades on a knife edge,
I feel fear bubbling in my stomach.
She is as unbalanced
as anyone that I have ever met.
I do not fear that she will cut herself
if she falls, we both know
she does that already.

Red ladder ripped into her arm;
her personal physical feedback forum.
Red ladders on her arm,
serpents in her life.
This is no game.

She tells me she won't say that vile, hated word,
so she just says, he vio-lat-ed her.
We both know what she means,
we both know how this works.

She talks, I listen.
She talks, I listen.
She cries, she screams, I listen.
Sometimes I talk. Sometimes she listens.
Sometimes I talk so she doesn't have to listen.

I'm not here to tell her things that she doesn't know.
I'm here to show her things she has always known.
She is broken, but never beyond repair.

I know a girl who skates. She
rollerblades on a knife edge.

Spare Change
Leon Priestnall

A young man. Late twenties. Handsome features that go unnoticed. He sits on the street. His back against the stone wall. Humans in herds busily walk past him. He has a board that reads

'I've been homeless for over a year. I feel invisible. Please, any change you can spare?'

Opposite, across the wide city centre street, a protest is occurring. Outside the bookstore. Placards and shouting voices. Fair play means fair pay.

A couple kiss in a stairwell near by.

On the concrete pavement, a trampled newspaper has a muddied footprint across Donald Trump's face.

'Has it come to this' by the streets rings in my head.

As I plough through a city I've lived in so long that I could stand in a single spot and it would spark a cinematic montage of different memories.

I plough through, caught in the grip of a severe anxiety, that goes unnoticed and seems reflected in the current state of world affairs.

Wondering about all the thoughts worthy of poetry that go unpublished, much more worthy than I, and also, if there's any change going spare?

Ten (X)
Scarlett Ward

I'm trying to smoke less.
That's why I only buy packs of
(I) Ten now,
and not twenty.
(II) Ten
To keep my mouth busy
When I'm at a complete loss for words
Because too many of them clamber at once for release.
(III) Ten,
For when lashing out at other people
isn't working to fix what hurts,
so I smoke the air I should have used to explain.
(IV) Ten,
To fill my chest with soot
in the hopes that flowers will grow out of my mouth
like technicolour gardens stuffed into my cavities.
(V) Ten
For diary pages folded away and never spoken of,
Tucked away into cupboard drawers
My wounds, my secrets, tucked, away into cupboard drawers.
(VI) Ten,
Is just enough to scald my mouth
and burn away those words
I spat at my mother in hate.
(VII) Ten
To keep my lungs inflated
when my heart drops heavy enough to collapse them
after seeing her crumple at words thrown at her
by a tongue that her own body grew.
(VIII) Ten
For when I realized how easy it is to hurt someone
When that someone reminds you so much of yourself.

The only Mother tongue I inherited is my mother's
inability to use it.
(IX) Ten
For times when all I want to do
is just to scream my apologies,
but her mouth is a cave of material that won't echo it back.
It's only sometimes,
I need those
(X) Ten.
I'm trying to smoke less.

Leaving The Nest
Ariya Larker

I perch at the end of your bed - like I always do - beside a snoozing Molly bear, whilst you chatter away about the usual family gossip.

Molly sleeps peacefully as I tickle behind her ears and I cannot retain the grin that bleeds across my visiting face, because she has erupted into a purring symphony.

We both know that she is happy when I am here.

I help you pick the outfit you will wear tonight and after a few agonising moments of pleading and reasoning, you convince me to do your make-up, though I know you will complain.

I tell you again what products I am using and explain where it must be applied, but you do not listen: I will always do it for you.

Work is forever unforgiving and your worn out body cries out for another holiday, but the mortgage still creeps through the floor boards and entwined with worries about the past and the future, your dreams mirror a repeated record of your many regrets.

I think about my husband, still working off the dent our wedding celebrations left in our accounts and how tired he always looks.

I think about the weekly letters I still bring to your room when I visit and see the same frowns tattooed across his forehead.

I think about how quiet the house must be now: both your children come and go.

I think about how you are the only person who lives here, as I descend heavily down the stairs and suddenly worry that you never use the chain on the front door.

I think about how you struggled to sleep when your children lived at home and worry about the echoing howls of night terrors knocking at your door and I tell myself that I should text more, call more, visit more...I feel that regret I know keeps you up at night.

Did we spend enough time together? Do I see you enough? Do I stay long enough? I always seem so eager to go, so eager to get back to my hardworking husband who longs to see his best friend after a gruelling day as an adult.

I feel like I'm torn, though I know neither one of you ever wants that for me.

The hardest aspect of humanity I have struggled to deal with so far, on my adventure, has been the spectrum of emotions I battle on a daily basis.

I hurt and I know you do too, but we will live and we will adapt to this change, because I will always be your daughter.

The In-Between Date
Nafeesa Hamid

I shaved until I was new born for this guy. Curled my hair cute behind my ears as my parents slept in the next room. Sprayed the Isi Miyaki that was saved for special occasions like Eid, across neck, wrists, anywhere else I could imagine his mouth, hands, tongue forging their place. Nivea moisturise peach-peel skin. Baggy t-shirt that dad got free from the National Lottery and pyjama shorts.

You creep into the garden turned on harder by the adrenaline of being found out; your brother is sleeping only meters away. You have left the back door unlocked. The boy who walks through the back gate is ginger, Reebok traccies and smiling with glaze-eyed testosterone. His hands, both, are dragging themselves up your chest finding something to hold on to, finding ripened nipples and making do, pinching and pulling you into him, your pyjama shorts limping unwillingly in the night's rain asking you what the hell you're doing. He moves one hand down and you move yours down and he's as hard as your dad's knuckles against your cheek when you were seven and you're as wet as your mother's tears when they found you at 5am when you were nine. And he is moving faster and you are moving faster and it is raining over both of you but who the fuck cares.
Yes. Yes. Yes.
He takes his yes other hand off your sore yes bloated yes breasts yes and slithers down yes and down yes and down yes and he's trying to push himself into your tight wetness yes and you are no panicking now no and mumbling no something about virgin no not done this no virgin please stop I'm a virgin stop please no stop. And he does.
You offer a blowjob instead. You go to bed still tasting of semen and sin, fighting the urge to chisel away the insides of your mouth.

I shaved until I was new born for this guy. I feel soft and old and torn and worn now. I do not reply to any of his Facebook messages. I do not answer his questions about who I want to be when I grow up.

I just want to stop being so woman.

Liberation
Yasmina Silva

if ever I should forget
how to untangle
the aggression
of
oppressive tongues
from my
hair

shave it.

then let it sprout
anew
from a place
of
liberation.

Reunion
Leah Atherton

Hello –
You're here.
And I have no idea how to talk to you.

Hi –
I've been choosing these words for years
In case they're the last ones we'll ever share.

How have you been?
There are lies I practiced in the mirror
until I almost believed them myself.

Yes I've been well –
I haven't stopped watching the moon
since you vanished.

Thank you;
Sometimes I wonder if
I imagined you.

I've been busy, you know–
I can map every freckle the sun has
put on your face since the last time
I kissed you.

What are you up to now?
Where do you go to that is off the map
of us you once drew on my palm?

Are you happy?
Did it hurt when you erased me?

How's your family?
I will never be able to un-know
the soft of you.

I'm glad you're doing well now.
There are letters I am afraid to write you
but you appear in so many poems
you've become an accent my mouth cannot un-learn.

Hello –
I have said good-bye to you so many times
I no longer trust the moon.
And you're here.

Future Clothes
Livi Pilkington

I sometimes wonder
We think so much about each other
Naked
That if these thoughts were fabricated
They would cover each inch of our bodies in silk.
Then maybe our grip over each other would slip.
Flesh would be ours to own.

I would wear crop tops in the summer
Because it's hot, because I like my midriff
The way it breaks the fall of fabric to fabric .
Stripes to denim.
Stripes to belly to denim.
-But you don't see that the way I do:
You see the non-existent ink on the button of my abdominal
That says, "I wish to be unbuttoned."
I do not.
I have bigger dreams.

If only I'd known when I bought my first bra,
That I'd spend the rest of my life worrying about straps
Because when they are red, not white
They can call to you like a bull in a rink of wandering eyes
I would've put the hanger down
And hung onto the straps of my backpack
Since when did my body become so sexualised?

I'll be the first to admit
That when I see a woman on the streets
In a bodycon dress and fishnet tights
A word crosses the lips of my mind
That holds such harsh sibilance
It shocks me as much as her dress may to passers-by

But then, I remember
This woman's agenda
Is not defined by where her skirt comes on her thighs
Nor is it anything to judge her by

Please, look
At my bright pink trousers.
I want them to meet your yellow co-odds.
Look at my deathly gallows tee.
Let's have a chat about Albus Dumbledore.
Heck, look at me in the these jeans.
I'm aware there is beauty in the female form
And I'm not condemning this.
Please, look
But don't touch,
Or call
Or think you have the right to.

We all wear so many layers you can't see:
I wear these porcelain gloves that say
Hold my hand before you take me off.
A hat that hides my head and the thoughts behind it
But can be removed if conditions are warm enough,
Heels that are strong and sexy
But cause me to tumble and fall.

So before you think about taking off someone's jeans,
know the threads the zipper can get caught on.
Take your time with their clothes and layers underneath,
Walk in their shoes a little
before you ask them to take off their socks.
And remember:
taking anyone's layers off,
Is not as easy as it looks.

Maleena
Ahsen Sayeed

You've drowned the sun in your Noor
And she's blinded.
Your thick curly locks sway me away like the green trees in my mind sway fears astray
i swear I'm sorry but
I was young and dumb and i didn't know right from wrong
And i swear you were the most beautiful thing I've ever set my cold dark eyes upon

Maleena i am guilt ridden 15 years on
How i didn't know your blood was stained with a promise -
Maleena i promise
I promise. I take an oath
That if i ever get to see your porcelain craft face -
Take my hand, hold it. I just wanted to track your growth but -

Your Moroccan sunrise cheeks and
Intergalactic Sunset eyes
Are every damn reason i live in memory but I'm blind

I ask god every bitter chilled night for a chance to cross mine with your path
Yet i know if i ever did id freeze so i stop

I'm on all 4s now more than ever when i think back to 2004
And how i was too small to comprehend the scent of chemicals pouring out of each pore
Which furthermore wanted me to be your friend even less than before

Maybe the 10 by 12 old carpet smell didn't really help
But i don't really know

Maybe sitting next to you amongst 28 other kids is one of the best choices I've ever made in life
But i don't really know
Maybe seeing your bold head over a 2 frame per second skype camera was more scarring than you'll ever know
Maybe this journey is part of a route
So i strap up and tie the lace on my left boot a bit tighter than last time with a question i ask why. why did you try to go?

Perhaps god wanted you back so soon that he realised
That my love is enough proof to keep you strong
Although I've wasted 15 damn straight years
I can wait another 15 damn straight years searching for you.

Perhaps seeing you on the brink of death
Is more than enough reason to stand in front of everyone and express it to my last breath

Maleena i take a vow that if
Somehow my soul could take me back and allow
To relive every last moment to gaze at yours i just would

Maleena cancer is so much more than a
Zodiac sign especially for you
Your ex disease lies dormant as i would cross seas to breathe the same stale air as you

Your illness is more than enough to kill us
And although it did I'm here 15 years on asking for forgiveness so please just let it go

That carbon filled covalent bonded sealed thing in your upper left part of your imprisoned dry bone thing that i wanna call diamond, see?

Maleena. Don't go. Don't leave me
Hopefully these clicks in this dim lit room is enough for you

to believe me

Your 24-karat skin purity is enough security to hide and shield your delicate impurities
Your voice is a charity
He's come back to bless me its Rumi
You're more than i see. And now i see
So clearly that it's kinda embarrassing
That though you may consider these breaths i take a waste of infinity

Maleena just know. Just know that
Though the last time i saw your moonlit face was in a crowded place
It was 6 years ago
It was 6 years ago and plenty of lovers have come and gone but you always stayed in the back of my mind like a love song.
Maleena your bewitched face has convinced me. You've convinced me.
When I've ever ceased to exist
Your face is the face of peace I'm convinced.
Maleena. You are peace personified.
And if it takes me to die
I've died
And if it takes me to cry
Oceans are dry in comparison
To each town and city there's a garrison in my heart
Or should i say soul because that's the level it'll take for me to reach you
I guess if this life is too short to reach you
Next time I'll comeback as a Hindu
Maybe your reincarnate soul will comeback as a butterfly
And i pray that i do too.

Maleena i think I've sorta seen you at your worst
And i don't mean that like a drake song
This is your song so have it

Seeing you go from playground
To bed-bound
Was more than my eyes could have it -
Hearing our teachers saying that you won't come back
I won't lie it kinda made me snap
But here we are.
And as far as I'm concerned you're living.
So live for the moments that were stolen away from you
Live and make all your wishes and dreams come true

If i could ever press mine
Against your winter wilted rose petal lips
I'd hold my breath a minute or two longer
In hopes that my kiss could give life. Or at least make you stronger.

So when i speak these words out loud
I stand proud and say
My best friend beat cancer.

Dis Black Womanhood
Amara Ranger

i think this black womanhood is so delicate sometimes. it almost makes me cry sometimes. it is so beautiful. i am so desperate for it to be preserved. i am so angry that it has ever been accused of anything, how dare you. how dare you all. we have given you everything. i'm sure of it. we have given you everything. we have hidden so much of ourselves and ironed and straightened ourselves up for you. our arms are heavy with your burdens. our hearts, my god our hearts, are quiet for our own worries and wail loudly for our sons, our daughters, our mothers. our eyes only hang low so that tears will not fall, we somehow cannot bare to be one tear lighter. we are mammy and girl. we are too woman and too masculine. too round bottomed or flat chested or too black. we are light and tiptoeing most days but we are too dark and easily mistaken as evil. i am tired of making you all jump for fear in the midst of trying not to show that i am a little fearful of you all. actually. you frighten me. you, will look god in her black face and dig and curse and shame and fill with pain and stir up anger. you play with the danger that you demonise. you frighten me. Whoever looked plainly at what was beautiful and giving and forced tears that would drown out the sounds or possibility of genuine ones from eyes that needed the water?

Noise
Dennis Muhirwa Nkurunziza

I could hear noise all around me! Screams, shrieks, shrill sounds that made me shiver,
sending shrapnel down my spine.
Fragments of a mind, which on some days was so void.
So, unwilling to reveal its contents to its own keeper.
Oh, the secrets it hid so well.
Buried beneath layers and layers of
Nothing much and it's okay.
Flirting with insanity and nooses, telling them how good we'd look together.
Cheating on God.
Cheating on myself like it was normal.
Acting like suppression actually made sense.
It had me tiptoeing around my thoughts
Never wanting to awaken these sleeping giants
Who would wreak havoc whenever they woke and they seemed to wake all at the same time.
I could hear a pin drop in a sea of regrets, the cries of we could've made it.
Never seemed loud enough! They were soft whispers that had to be found by not trying.
They were sweet nothings that brought you closer and closer to the edge.
You see, self-depreciation takes its toll.
This world can be all sunshine and roses, but the sun's rays can cause heat-stroke,
And roses have thorns but that shouldn't keep you up at night.
Every piece I write is me trying to escape this prison built for one.
In a way hoping for redemption from my very own Shawshank.
I am just a 5 ft 11 feather filled fence that looks a whole lot like stone, my bark is a lot worse than my bite and my bark isn't

much to begin with.
I am an open book written in a language I barely understand.
It is why I write.
Write about how I decided which chapter was going to be the last in this story.
Write about how God had other plans.
Write about the horrors living in the dark corners of our minds that we never want to face
But who always want to face us.
Who always seem to stare back at us when we look in the mirror.
Who make mockeries of our dreams and tell us.
All we can choose between is the devil and the deep blue sea.
The number of people fighting depression alone is too damn high!
If that is how you choose to deal, I will respect that.
But I am human just like you, that alone makes us connected enough for me to care.
That alone makes you my brother.
My sister.
If you need someone to listen I'm here, there are safe spaces all around you.
The beauty of love is in its ability to heal all, don't tell me about time.
This right here Is my testimony.
Every morning you wake up, be thankful.
Every night you make it back to your bed, be thankful.
Every breath you take, be thankful.
Hold on to the ones you love like they are the last breath of fresh air you'll ever take.
Take that last breath every day.
Let it get you out of bed in the morning.
If you think no one loves you, treat yourself like you are the love of your life!
And show love to everyone around you.
I could hear noise all around me, screams, shrieks, shrill sounds that made me shiver.

But I could also hear happiness, the mending of broken hearts. The laughter of a child, the excitement in an old person's voice as they relived their best memories.
I absolutely love this life.
I love the feeling I get in church when God is taking over.
I love the strangers who smile at me on the street because in those two seconds
I have seen every beautiful thing in their life and I just want to see more but probably never will.
I love that the curvature of your smile tells more about you than you think.
And the look in your eyes when you think no one is looking is a story I would love to read over and over.
I love watching people become the best version of themselves.
But above all else, I love that I am no longer chasing hearts...
I am just trying to be love. God is taking this noise and turning it into something worth seeing,
Something worth listening to. I am finally letting myself become my version beautiful.

Brown Voices Amongst White Noises
Aliyah Begum

Our voices are not heard until it is said we are shouting too loudly.
Why?
Because our history is rich
Until it is tippexed out of the textbooks.
Because our advances in science are not useful,
Unless they are discovered by a white man.
Because the soft curl of our mother tongue
Falls harshly on closed ears.
Because our skin is brown,
While their fake tan is 'glowing and bronzed'.
Because my eyebrows are bushy,
Until a model makes it the new trend.
Because my headscarf is 'oppressive'
Until someone wears it on Vogue.
Because we are irrelevant
Until a new curry house opens in Edgbaston:
Authentic dishes, no spice,
Uncle Ben is the saviour of rice.

Because we are ignored
Until a scapegoat is needed for those who pervert our beliefs
For their own twisted needs.
This is wrong, this goes without saying.
Yet it is the only thing we are scolded for not saying.

Because they have selective hearing;
Taking fragments of our voices,
Rearranging to make sentences they like
The ones picked out of the white noise.

Number 6
Kamil Mahmood

Doors slam themselves awake
Knees scuttle steps tiptoeing insects.
I haste along the thick of it
Pace to a place that'll displace me
Out of the routine
White flag a bus that will bring colour to this grey.
In mind's eye spark hills, brooks and green halls.
Surely the sullied hull of this ship will last but touch wood
the Polaroids don't develop too fast
Force like fist down timid throat
Headphones that match the genre of this moment.
I'm running
No faster than 30mph
And amber lights are contemplation
Red lights meditation
Vibrating laps and sweat clothed backs the sensation
This microcosm might cost £4.20
But this trip could be the day saver
Stay in your own lane
Poles and pockets
Foreign tongues wafting their scents
Breeding the environment with their own
And in a split second it's not a bus
It's a boat or a PIA aeroplane. And it's time share.
Hijabs and turbans and crucifixes
Masjids meet gurdwaras greet churches
Side by side in tessellation
Unknown in their Piloted utopia
On a road that's more like an aorta
I'm going somewhere
But the destination won't live up to this situation.

Hobbies Include:
Hannah Swings

My fear is a hiker holding a flare gun during a forest fire
Camped in a crease of my mind
Last thing standing and furthest from help:
Fear is the 'Z' in Scrabble.
I'm scared of waxwork eyes
Mountain range knuckles
And metal clutched so tightly to skin it changes how it feels to hold silk.
I'm scared of losing you, not losing myself
Because this happens so often, more often, more recently
Try and cling to corners, sides
Because everything in the middle is muddled
With good intentions like a jigsaw puzzle,
Half an hour old.
I'm scared that I have failed the people before me
Who built this city of a thousand trades
Ready for me to run it
Who would not expect a Cluedo whodunit
Of the character I'd end up playing.
In a land formed on 'Forward'
I'm always checking what's behind me
But I've finally cracked the code:
We unpick stitches without knowing what they're holding together.
Because we weren't taught the craft of fixing
Instead of throwaway and trends
We need 'make do and mend'.

Darn the holes cut from self-criticism into compliments
Knit reasons to stay alive into quilts
Slept under by lovers that will stay longer than the bad thoughts.
Cross-stitch across my clothes

So I can drape kisses around my shoulders
So tired from the weight of this world
But more so to prove a point
(No needle pun intended)
That metal held tightly can change how it feels to hold silk
Yet sometimes for the better.

Withering
Adjei Dsane

a collection of lucid fears
each night i would greet the mirror like a criminal in a line up
to love me was to love a living breathing symptom of sleepless nights
for monsters lingered in the depths of my mind
to the fog and Bacardi depression invited cousin anxiety
all night house music played though at home i cannot say i felt
i prayed to escape the skin i was born within
aside i pushed my plate having eaten two bites of rice and peas
teeth marks on my brass knuckles greased in cocoa butter
into selfie camera and glass i stared
trying to find something worth calling pretty
pulling flesh to belong to another body.
i boy that became skeleton and
vanished   into   thin   air.

My Friend's Grandmother Is A Socialist
Ahlaam Moledina

Another time, she called The State
a caricature,
a dramatisation for the purpose of
entertainment. She said that
he sits at the top of his tower,
watches like a hungry stray
that eyes your barbecue,
and like your senses in the July
heat, your allegiance to him is
distorted.
We're like dust mites in sunbeams,
she said,
we float above the earth
hypnotised and happy
(or spellbound and angry?)
guided by the rays of expediency
that drip, viscous, like sweet honey,
into our eyes, enhancing our tea.
We attempt to make our marks on
the grievances of the ground
without ever having been there.
We soar, she said, immune to
earthquakes, to floods-
liberation lies in submission (to the
wind or) to him,
(we'd succumb to the pull either way)
so we spread our bliss, conquer
land after land with an iron fist of
humility and good will. We will
never let our wings touch the
ground but we are benevolent.

Before every caricature is an artist.
We will enforce harmony, she sighs
over her scarlet knitting,
we will enforce peace
without ever having been there.

Monday The 11th of December 2017. 21:05
Ciona Nankervis

The pavements are laden with meringue
Haphazard slather smeared along the road.
Trees, like proud antlers, highlighted by the season's bliss
Stretch deep into the charcoal sky.

There is an eeriness surrounding snow at night
Enveloping, smothering,
It muffles sound and sight-
Deadening, yet still illuminating.
Into a cloak of dusty treacle
The emotionless throw of LED bulbs
reflects
Turning all to a spectral landscape.

Extinct
Jasmine Gardosi

In the year 3020
they went to the UK to excavate.

It was like Pompeii all over again
and this time, the ash preserved nothing.

Well, they found one thing.

Beneath the crumbs of a pre-fab school
though what used to be a locked door
in a cabinet, bolted to the wall and floor
wrapped in a waterproof plastic seal

was a handful of booklets.

It was clear this was the pinnacle of English literature,
so safely capsuled for discovery.
And these documents, the sole clue to the 21st Century
were each entitled

Exam paper. Unit 1B.

The evidence implied this was a gripping fictional series
adored by the nation
authored by the mysterious Ed Excel.

The discoverers deciphered characters
like Sarah, the protagonist of Mathematics Non-Calculator
who, it reads, 'Has 16 beads in her bag.
Three of them are blue.
What is the probability
she'll pull one of these out?'

What a genius
the scholars said.
This writer leaves us with questions.
He can admit to not knowing all the answers.

The graph of Gopal's rising heart rate
the parallelogram in Figure 8c
the cartoon of Sarah's famous bag of beads
were another clue:

these were picture books -
they were meant for children

designed to keep them up at bedtime
and they did.

Designed to have them hooked since the start of high school
and they did.

Too bad the apocalypse
wiped out all signs of us.

Gentrification Poem
Joe Cook

Gentrifying rampaging
Like Godzilla in Tokyo
small coffee shops crushed
By tall tax dodgers to go
Losing what's unique
Shape shifting like mystique
Same image on repeat
Like Warhol's paintings
Cities transforming
Deceptions
Conquering cybertron
Small business gone
Two sides to gentrified
Like Harvey dent
How the moneys spent
Have to CPR the heart of the city
When we're buying cereal bowls for £5.50
Corn flakes
Bran flakes
Piss takes
If that's the route regeneration
And innovation takes us
Cheerios
To the city of culture status

Aerosol cans breath life
On bricks of forgotten industry
Reincarnation through illustration
Like rock n roll
They white was the wall
Don't own the streets
Like losing in monopoly
Sacrificed

to luxury property
Like bailiffs at the door
Taking everything of value
But still want to sell you
Reverse Robin Hood
Giving to the rich
Taking from the poor
Big city plan
Edward Scissor hands
Dishing out the cuts
Can give the city an airbrush
They even moved the Iron man
Big business like Tony Stark
All praise to Primark
Sweatshop monastery
Sale on the scenery
They don't know the cities struggles and troubles
Watch from their towers above
Stone cold like gargoyles
Might be on the rise
But who's left behind

You can do up a cars exterior
Can give it a spoiler, rims and fresh paint tones
But if the engine is inferior
And its got a motor
Like the car from the Flintstones
It won't run
get you where you want to be
We need to take care of the smaller nuts and bolts
The mechanics of this city
A souped up vehicle
But the soup kitchens still full
The valuable and vulnerable components
Rather than a makeover
Repair those that are broken

Her (v2)
Seunfunmi Tinubu

She tastes like cinnamon apples and peace of mind. Her laugh brings my heart rate down from stratospheric levels and momentary calm encases me. She's a gift. Not the kind of gift that you haphazardly buy for your cousin's wedding the night before, but the kind that you plan for months in advance so that you can appreciate the pure joy that explodes in your mother's iris when you give it to her. I wasn't lost before she came along, I was just fine. Just fine is fine until you find someone that turns the most mundane activity into a memory that makes stupid grins creep across my face during midday meetings at work.

If I had one eighth of her talent, maybe I'd be able to truly express how I feel about her. 'I love you' is too simple but my pen lacks the magic that hers possesses. She turns ten words into a definitive statement on the human condition while I make a rudimentary grocery list.

The words that cross my mind, when you cross the room
A flower in bloom, you are the epitome of grace, perfection

eggs

bread

milk

strawberry orange jello

chocolate chip cookies

'I love you'

I painted it in big blue letters across the bedroom wall. My failed letters graced the floor like seeds that would only reap more awful literature. Her eyes were teary and she made her away across the room, into my arms and told me that she loved me too. Her smile, those perfect white teeth offset by that dark brown skin, had my heart ready to explode. We made love and it was carefree and imperfect and we laughed a lot. Her lean body, wrapped around mine, the two of us moving as one, her cries pushing me further until we rolled over the edge, literally and figuratively. My shoulder is a little bruised but I'd fall a hundred times for moments like that.

Now she's sleeping, and I'm sitting and the world is quiet and the room is dark. An angel is a few feet away from me but I've learned to compartmentalize my amazement and simply accept that I've never been more blessed. I used to be lonely and crave companionship, like a junkie craves a needle. Those late nights, wondering why women that wouldn't notice me if I walked into their room on fire didn't love me. I am no longer addicted to being made whole by someone else. I was just fine before her, if there ever is a time after her I will be just fine. In these late hours when the world is stuck between night and morning and God is sleepily fumbling for his alarm clock, I am no longer alone.

Theatre Is Not For Us
Jacob Crutchley and Zeddie

Theatre is not for me
Bourgeois bureaucracy that made me feel I cannot see paths available to me
15 years old, high dreams of being on stages and starring roles
A Drama teacher's faith keeping me from falling off and being on parole
Pushing
encouraging
filling this head with aspirations telling me all it took was old fashioned hard work and dedication.
I don't blame her she put her faith in an energy source even she didn't understand
The card I dealt her was not the only one in hand.

Surrounded by a circle where theatre was taboo
The only thing that mattered was a 20 bag and who looked the oldest to buy the booze
Notions of being a bad man dictating what I do, misguided youth without the faintest clue of how to progress theses secret dreams.
That I came to realise were simply unaffordable.
The 4th wall stays strong and keeps people like me out.
Theatre is not for me

Theatre is not for me,
Growing up in a place where I was the minority
I was encouraged to go for some roles, the same roles
 You know the ones that aesthetically suited me,
Dancing in preconceptions on playing the "hood girl"
Whilst dreaming in the disproportionate reality of Brecht,
You see I could relate to one, but not the other but the one i should have related to didn't match
"You'll go far because there's not many like you"

You have got the look.
But you didn't see me.
Back then that's what i clung on to
Because that's all I knew
I know now that
theatre is not for me

Theatre is not for me
The 4th wall financial barrier of joining a youth theatre.
The 4th wall of social stigma sticking to me as I try to relate to
classics texts that I could just about read.
Feeling isolated on a lonely desert island stuck with a language
I couldn't understand
Palm trees of protagonists drawing my hand into confusion
Going to college with a cohort who didn't get where I was coming from
Couldn't understand my speech patterns and use of slang,
hyper energy drum & bass gun finger hand signs
For them I was a walking stereotype of half-truths & media lies
In their eyes I was every single thing their parents despised.
I was done, fell off the ladder and entered the graft with new
dreams and aspirations centred around generating cash.
3 jobs deep, night shift day shift rinse and repeat
shifting and stacking theatre to the back of my mind
Eat sleep work repeated process of the rat race making
aspirations harder to find
buried deep down inside my subconscious mind
because Theatre is not for me.

Theatre is not for me,
I grew up and out of expectations
Finally breaking free into spaces i could call my own
Possessing fragments of dreams that re-wrote the stories
That didn't include my perspective
Refusing to conform to the stigmas and the meanings behind
the words because those words had no meaning to me
Battling our ideologies with the ideologies of capitalism

and learning about political histories
It was inherent that the spaces i thought i had the keys to
Triple locked and built walls for people like me
We swim in narratives that are "untrue"
Stories that are too much and too hard and too graphic
Both those are the narratives that are only too true for some
And i have met them
And now you play them but only parts
Using systems and stories to capture the essence of them
But the essence was and is life, hard times,
You can practice and it can be perfect
But perfection without essence is meaningless to some
A few,
Us
Theatre is not for me

Theatre is not for me.
I had never seen any stories that really spoke to me
Not 6 degrees of separation from a character's strife
analysing complex plot lines to draw conclusions to my life
I had never just seen an engaging production and felt that it was right.
Times change
3 years pass the bubbling dreams and aspirations begin come back.
Surpass the need for cold hard cash
Time to make one quick last hack and slash to make theatre apart of my life
Drama school applications, government grants getting familiar with student finance
Rock up
day one
feel out of my depth
Everybody talking about the breadth of experience with performing arts
with all associated laughs and larks.
"And you Jacob tell us about your past?"

Teenage years of tear away trouble
Late teens of drug dealing bubbles
Away day violence football fights
Copious amounts of drug taking late into the night
Nothing special to be honest mate pretty normal right?
Shocked faces sticky stigmas attached to my world
Fear and intrigue by peers that I took to heart
drifting feelings of isolation as my lonely Island began
to depart
feelings and misrepresentation just kept saying that
Theatre is not for me.

Theatre is not for me
I am tearing down libraries
Breaking through the one-sided stories
Losing myself in books and dark crevices of new age realities
 tucked away collecting dust in rooms that are
Sealed shut
Why do you ask?
They uncover stories similar to mine
But they are too few
Conversing with one too many with
Who whisper their narratives in secret
Questioning their reality
Who are now breaking through their whispers
Screaming they
No longer will they worship pages on a book as if it were sacred
For this is more than one story
Our eyes are opening
People are reclaiming
And spaces are changing
For they are burst open to people who see themselves
Because they are no longer stories
These are documentations of the everyday to mundane to the
brilliant
Taking erasers to the text books to reshape the preconceptions
to make them

Just about right
Breaking through stereotypes
Because the boxes that were built became too tight
There's a renaissance in the air
People are building from the ground up
Saying that theatre is not for me

Theatre is not for me,
Drama school lecturers challenging my everyday beliefs
built up guilt
guard dropping
Letting people into my world to see who I really am
A young boy from Birmingham in a full suit of armour
who's only teenage escape was being involved in drama, of every kind
But never mind I'm naked now for all to see
This is the moment I thank those who had faith
2013 the year of my future starting
stigmas washed off that lonely island
colonised by the stark reality of dream chasing.
I need to refresh
change my perspective
be a cliché and see the world and undergo some self-reflection.
I slowly to start to feel this world is a long way from perfection
2 years of being abroad and deep contemplation
Cementing who I really was
realising where I wanted to be was this this city making a difference
Using my art as a weapon
I wanted to wage war
start a cause
pick apart this industry and highlight its flaws
I started to think about what my drama teacher from school thought she saw
I started to think about Lecturers that took me back to my core beliefs
Stripping back my Brum Town urban armour

That didn't let people know who I really was
I started to get it
Hard work and dedication wasn't a tactic to pursue
It was allowing myself to be patient for truth.
Theatre is not for me

Theatre is not for me,
I look back the work that has been done
But it's not enough
The movement is growing too fast
And the division is getting deeper
Monologues re-written into acceptable text
And now there's a
new task at hand to be met
For unlearning what has been taught
Whilst learning the new
Has created a new dialogue
That forces to merge the two
And now the spaces forcing separation
see us
They include more than one or two or just a few
For they want the same things too
As the world is changing direction
We will move forward
Multiculturalism is taking spaces
Audiences are transforming
As knowledge is expanding in both size and colour
No longer saying
Theatre is not for me

Theatre is not for me
2016 the opportunity arose and I grasped it with both hands
Always looking back
I have the golden ticket
I feel like Charlie.
Opportunities carved out from honesty
Now I walk the corridors of institutions

Making artistic contributions to fuel this city
And now I see a different side
Tick boxes
bums on seats
I'm still searching for something that just speaks
Engrossed in a world that has been chased for so long
Surrounded by people that show nothing but love
But still
I can't escape the words
I constantly stare at my own reflection
Green eyes of a 15-year-old boy gazing right back
Looking over my shoulder
All I see
Big red letters

Theatre is not for Us

The Jam
Sipho Eric Dube

Maya had the 'Jam'
Langston had the 'Jam'
Abel Meeropol, roped southern ropes into song.

Freedom had a voice - now freedom hides behind art.

But the Poet loves the Painter

And the Polymath Loves the 'Jam'.

And the revolutionary,
Though young,
Fights fire with cool
Prejudice with style.
Melts genres, onto canvas, to engage new gatherings.
In this is the changer who knows other changers.
In this is the thinker, who loves the heart of one.
This is all one -
So proudly and loudly
The 'Jam' continues on.

THE POETS (IN ORDER OF APPEARANCE)

Amerah Saleh - Website: www.amerahsaleh.co.uk
Nadia Ghazan - Instagram: @Khushimiri
Polarbear - Twitter: @homeofpolar
Giovanni Spoz Esposito - Twitter: @SpozPoet
Kavita Kler - Tumblr: http://log-a-stellus.tumblr.com/tagged/mywriting
Deanna Rodger - Website: https://www.deannarodger.co.uk/
Nyanda Foday - Twitter: @YoungPoetOfBrum
Lexia Tomlinson - Twitter: @LexiaLegend
Saidatu Odutayo - Twitter: @Freespirit_Ekun
Dawn Grant
Casey Bailey - Website: www.baileysrapandpoetry.com
Leon Priestnall - Facebook: Leon Poetry
Scarlett Ward - Instagram: @scarlett.ward
Ariya Larker - Twitter: @Ariyaaa94
Nafeesa Hamid - Twitter: @NafeesaHamid
Yasmina Silva - Twitter: @Yasmeeener
Leah Atherton - Twitter: @AthertonPoetry
Livi Pilkington - Twitter: @LiviPilkington
Ahsen Sayeed - Instagram: @Juniorahsen
Amara Ranger - Twitter: @Amara_Ranger
Dennis Muhirwa Nkurunziza - Twitter: @Dante_DMN
Aliyah Begum
Kamil Mahmood - Twitter: @TheKamikazi
Hannah Swingler - Website: www.hannahswings.com
Adjei Dsane - Website: https://adjeisun.wordpress.com/
Ahlaam Moledina - Twitter: @_Ahlaamm
Ciona Nankervis - Website: www.punjabiteachocolatecake.wordpress.com
Jasmine Gardosi - Website: www.jasminegardosi.com
Joe Cook - Twitter: @JoeCook
Seunfunmi E. Tinubu - Twitter: @TinubuTweets
Jacob Crutchley - Twitter: @JayCrutchley
Zeddie - Twitter: @ZeddieStage
Sipho Eric Dube

Find bios for all the poets in the anthology here:
www.beatfreeks.com/poetry-jam

THANK-YOUS

There are so many people to thank. The most important one is to everyone who has ever turned up on the first Thursday of the month to listen, share, host or curate Poetry Jam as a safe space. Thank you, from the bottom of our hearts. There are a few key milestones that people and spaces have helped with so to be short and concise:

- Thank you to Urban Coffee Company for taking a chance in 2013 on a group of unruly young people with wild dreams and louder voices.
- Thank you to Java Lounge for taking us in when we needed a home.
- Thank you to Impact Hub Birmingham for hosting an incredible fourth birthday and for not making us leave.
- Thank you to 200 Degrees for giving us space to expand, we are proud to call you home for Poetry Jam.
- Big thanks to Giovanni 'Spoz' Esposito for donating the original Poetry Jam PA equipment.
- Thank you to all the baristas who worked those late shifts and were forced to listen to poetry. We hope you were inspired by some, or all.
- Thank you to Hentiyah Hukaptah (Najite Phoenix) for letting us print the first Poetry Jam flyer on the back of yours.
- To all the photographers and videographers who captured moments that will go down in history.
- Thank you to Rishi Bhardwaj for initiating the Poetry Jam brand and to our Bradley Morrison for making it pop.
- Thank you to Town Hall Symphony Hall for giving us such a beautiful space to host our almighty fifth birthday.
- Thank you to Verve Poetry Press for launching with this anthology.

You are all magic!

THE BEATFREEKS COLLECTIVE

Founded in February 2013 with the launch of Poetry Jam, the Beatfreeks Collective is a group of companies using creativity for good, based in the heart of Birmingham.

Society is a BIG place and it faces some big problems. But it also has huge potential, more than we can imagine. We fundamentally believe there is space to craft a new world whilst working to improve the one we have. That's why we've created a collective of companies using creativity for good; platforms for the art activists and the entrepreneurs.

At the heart of our work is a movement of people using creativity to challenge the world to be better. Our community is made up of artists, activists, entrepreneurs, designers, technologists, researchers and more.

YOUNG GIANT: A youth engagement agency building 'Institutions of the Future' through harnessing the power of youth; we help companies and young people to connect.

DOINK: A Do and Think Tank humanising data through creativity to tell extraordinary stories and facilitate better decisions.

FREE RADICAL: An art activism platform empowering young people to tell stories about themselves, the world and how they fit together (or not).

www.beatfreeks.com
@Beatfreeks
@YoungGiantUK
@FreeRadicalUK
@DoinkTank

www.vervepoetrypress.com
@VervePoetryPres
mail@vervepoetrypress.com